T0396955

CHRISTMAS

BY EMMA KAISER

Core Library

An Imprint of Abdo Publishing
abdobooks.com

Cover image: The annual Macy's Thanksgiving Day Parade in New York City features Santa Claus on a Christmas-themed parade float.

abdobooks.com

Published by Abdo Publishing, a division of ABDO, PO Box 398166, Minneapolis, Minnesota 55439. Copyright © 2024 by Abdo Consulting Group, Inc. International copyrights reserved in all countries. No part of this book may be reproduced in any form without written permission from the publisher. Core Library™ is a trademark and logo of Abdo Publishing.

Printed in the United States of America, North Mankato, Minnesota.
102023
012024

THIS BOOK CONTAINS RECYCLED MATERIALS

Cover Photo: Andrew Burton/Getty Images News/Getty Images
Interior Photos: iStockphoto, 4–5, 45; Shutterstock Images, 7, 18–19, 23, 34–35, 38, 39, 43; Red Line Editorial, 8; Chuta Kooanantkul/Shutterstock Images, 10–11; M&N/Alamy, 13; Ika Rahma H./Shutterstock Images, 15; Fine Art Images/Heritage Images/Hulton Fine Art Collection/Getty Images, 17; Freedom Studio/Shutterstock Images, 21; Kara Gebhardt/Shutterstock Images, 24; Hulton Archive/Hulton Royals Collection/Getty Images, 26–27; Lebrecht Music & Arts/Alamy, 29; Bettmann/Getty Images, 31; Universal History Archive/Universal Images Group/Getty Images, 32; Aleksandar Jankovic/E+/Getty Images, 36

Editor: Laura Stickney
Series Designer: Ryan Gale

Library of Congress Control Number: 2023939652

Publisher's Cataloging-in-Publication Data

Names: Kaiser, Emma, author.
Title: Christmas / by Emma Kaiser
Description: Minneapolis, Minnesota: Abdo Publishing, 2024 | Series: History of holidays and festivals | Includes online resources and index.
Identifiers: ISBN 9781098292584 (lib. bdg.) | ISBN 9798384910527 (ebook)
Subjects: LCSH: Holidays--Juvenile literature. | Fasts and feasts--Juvenile literature. | Christmas--Juvenile literature. | Christmas--History--Juvenile literature.
Classification: DDC 394.2663--dc23

CONTENTS

CELEBRATING CHRISTMAS

Ari wakes up early on the morning of December 25. Her little brother, Casey, is shaking her awake. "Do you think Santa came last night?" he asks her. Ari rubs her eyes. "Why don't we go find out?" she says. Casey pulls Ari out of bed. From outside Ari's bedroom window, they can see that it snowed last night. They run downstairs.

In Ari and Casey's living room, a large evergreen tree is strung with colorful electric lights. Red and green stockings hang from

Many people exchange gifts on the morning of Christmas Day, before breakfast. But some people open gifts on Christmas Eve.

the fireplace mantel. Under the tree are gifts wrapped in pretty paper and bows. When the rest of Ari and Casey's family wakes up, they all sit around the tree and exchange gifts. Ari grins when she opens up a new set of paints and paintbrushes.

Later in the day, Ari's grandparents, aunts, uncles, and cousins come over. The house smells like turkey, potatoes, and stuffing. Ari's mom made homemade sugar cookies and pumpkin pie for dessert. After dinner, Ari and Casey

PERSPECTIVES

CHRISTMAS CHEER

Studies show that people are more cheerful around Christmastime. Canadian psychologist Dr. Patrick Keelan says it's not just the decorations and lights that make people happy. Christmas is a time for family and togetherness, which increases happiness. Keelan says, "Holidays allow for many people to have more enjoyable social interactions with friends and family." Christmas can also bring back positive memories from childhood. This makes people nostalgic. For others, it's a time to celebrate their religion. These meaningful experiences produce feelings of happiness.

decorate gingerbread houses with frosting, candy canes, and gumdrops. They argue over which one is the best.

When Ari goes to bed that night, snow is falling outside her window again. She falls asleep easily this time. She thinks this might be her favorite Christmas yet.

CHRISTMAS AROUND THE WORLD

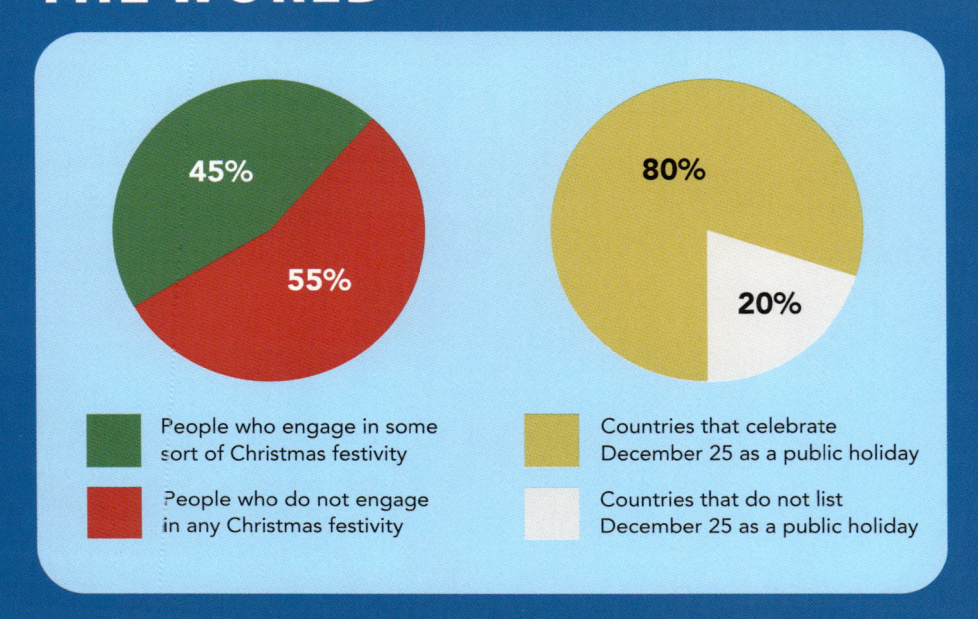

45%

55%

80%

20%

People who engage in some sort of Christmas festivity

People who do not engage in any Christmas festivity

Countries that celebrate December 25 as a public holiday

Countries that do not list December 25 as a public holiday

Many people worldwide engage in some sort of Christmas festivity. Many countries also celebrate Christmas as a public holiday. Based on the charts above, what can you tell about the popularity of Christmas?

A GLOBAL HOLIDAY

People all over the world celebrate Christmas. For Christians, it is an important religious holiday. It marks the birth of Jesus Christ. Jesus was a spiritual teacher whom Christians believe to be the son of God. Christians often attend church services on Christmas.

But Christians are not the only people who celebrate Christmas. For thousands of years, people have also celebrated it in nonreligious ways. For many, Christmas is a whole season of activities, from gift giving to decorating trees. One modern Christmas tradition is the figure of Santa Claus—a bearded man in a red suit who delivers gifts in a sleigh pulled by reindeer.

Christmas has a very rich history. What began as a winter festival became closely linked with the early Christian church. Over time, different cultures developed their own unique Christmas traditions.

THE YULE LADS OF ICELAND

In Iceland, there is a legend about trolls called the Yule lads, or *Jólasveinar*. It's said that during December, the Yule lads make their way down from the mountains. For 13 nights, 13 different Yule lads come bringing surprises. This lasts from December 12 to December 24. Children leave their shoes out on their doorsteps for the Yule lads. If the children have been good, the Yule lads leave a gift or treat in their shoes. If they've been naughty, the Yule lads leave rotten potatoes.

THE WINTER SOLSTICE

The winter solstice marks the shortest day and longest night of the year. In the Northern Hemisphere, or the half of Earth above the equator, the winter solstice usually falls on December 21 or 22. It occurs when the Northern Hemisphere is tilted the farthest distance away from the sun. Leading up to the solstice, days get shorter and colder. After the solstice, the days get longer again.

The winter solstice occurs because of how the planet tilts and rotates. But it has also

Stonehenge, an ancient monument in England, was built to align with the sunset on the winter solstice. The site may have been used for winter solstice feasts and celebrations.

PERSPECTIVES

THE SOLSTICE AND STONEHENGE

Stonehenge is a structure made up of stones near Salisbury, England. It was built around 2500 BCE. The people who built the stones arranged them to perfectly align with the winter and summer solstices. When the sun sets on the winter solstice, the light shines between the center stones. This was likely a way for ancient people to mark the changing of seasons. Today, people still gather at Stonehenge to watch the solstice. It reminds people of those who came before them. In 2022, Sam MacDonald took the day off work to visit Stonehenge for the winter solstice. She said that after watching the solstice, she "can believe that this winter won't last forever. Spring will come."

been seen as a day for rebirth and celebration. People have celebrated the winter solstice for thousands of years. Winter solstice celebrations existed long before Christmas became a holiday. They existed before Jesus was born. Many solstice traditions influenced how people celebrate Christmas.

WINTER SOLSTICE CELEBRATIONS

Since ancient times, different cultures

Yule logs were traditionally large logs or even whole tree trunks. They would be chopped down, hauled inside to the fireplace, and burned for 12 days.

have celebrated the winter solstice with feasting and festivals. Scandinavia is an area of northern Europe that includes Denmark, Norway, and Sweden. Thousands of years ago, Scandinavian people took part in a solstice celebration called Yule. The earliest mention of Yule is found in the writings of English historian Bede, dating from the 700s CE. Yule marked the rebirth of the sun. It was a time to celebrate new beginnings. One tradition was a Yule log, a large wooden log that burned throughout the festival. People also exchanged gifts and decorated evergreen trees with berries, pinecones, or fruit. The term "Yuletide" was first used in 1475 to describe "the season of Yule." Eventually, it was used to describe the time around Christmas.

In China, Dongzhi is a celebration that marks the arrival of winter. It falls between December 21 and December 23. It's believed to have begun over 2,000 years ago as a harvest festival. Workers returned from the fields and enjoyed the harvest with feasting. Some workers were given the day off. It was a time for families to gather and pay respects to their ancestors. They celebrated with *tangyuan*, a type of sweet rice ball. Many people in China continue to celebrate Dongzhi.

Tangyuan are usually made from rice flour and water. They are often stuffed with a filling, such as red bean or sesame paste, and served in a sweet syrup.

SATURNALIA

The Romans had one of the most extravagant winter solstice celebrations. Their festival was called Saturnalia. Roman historian Livy wrote that Saturnalia was first celebrated in the 500s BCE, but historians believe it started much earlier. Saturnalia honored Saturn, the Roman god of agriculture. Agriculture is the practice of farming. At first, the festival lasted for only one day. Later, it became a weeklong celebration leading up to the winter solstice. It was one of the most widely celebrated festivals in Rome.

BIRTH OF THE SUN GOD

Mithras is an ancient god who was first worshipped in Persia, an area that is now the country of Iran. He was known as the sun god. Mithras's birthday was said to be December 25. Over time, worship of Mithras spread to Rome. It was popular among the Romans to celebrate Mithras's birthday as a holiday. Before Christmas was declared a holiday, December 25 was one of Rome's holiest days.

Most businesses were closed during Saturnalia. People took time off from work and school. Enslaved people were temporarily freed and allowed to say or do what they wanted. People had parties, drank wine, and exchanged gifts. They decorated their homes with greenery and lights. Eventually, people in Rome would celebrate Christmas at the same time as Saturnalia. Some historians think Saturnalia celebrations influenced the date chosen for Christmas.

In ancient Rome, Saturnalia was a time for fun and parties. People feasted, played games, and wore colorful clothing. It was popular to exchange gifts of candles and holly.

EXPLORE ONLINE

Chapter Two discusses winter solstice celebrations. The website below goes into more depth about how Earth's position in the solar system affects the seasons. What new information did you learn from the website? What are other ways people around the world experience the winter solstice?

WHAT'S THE WINTER SOLSTICE?

abdocorelibrary.com/christmas

EARLY CHRISTIAN CELEBRATIONS

For Christians, Christmas is a celebration of Jesus's birth. Christians believe Jesus came to Earth as the son of God. The Christian Bible says Jesus was born to the Virgin Mary. She gave birth to him in a stable in Bethlehem, located in what is now Palestine, in about 4 BCE. Angels revealed the news of Jesus's birth to shepherds nearby. There were also three Magi, which means "wise men" or priests. They came from the East to bring Jesus gifts. The Magi brought Jesus gold, along

Artistic depictions of the Nativity often feature baby Jesus lying in a manger, Mary and Joseph, shepherds, and wise men. Barn animals such as oxen and donkeys may also be included.

19

with frankincense and myrrh. These were expensive materials used as perfume and precious oil.

Jesus was a real person who grew up to be a spiritual teacher. He was killed by the Roman government between 30 and 33 CE. Christians believe that Jesus rose from the dead and came back to life after three days. They believe he rose into heaven. For more than 300 years after Jesus's death, the early Christian church did not celebrate his birth. Some church leaders opposed recognizing the birth date of Jesus. They thought people should focus on Jesus's death and resurrection. But the first Christmas celebration took place in Rome on December 25 in 336 CE.

The Bible says Jesus performed miracles such as turning water into wine and restoring a blind man's eyesight. His teachings focused on forgiveness, compassion, and faith in God.

WHY DECEMBER 25?

The Bible does not say what exact day Jesus was born. But people have theories about why December 25 became the chosen date. Early church historian Sextus Julius Africanus believed Jesus's conception took place on March 25. This was thought to be the date of Jesus's death. Some believed Jesus's death and conception occurred on the same day. A typical pregnancy is nine months long, and nine months from March 25 is December 25.

Others believe December 25 was chosen partly because of Rome's winter solstice celebrations. At that

PERSPECTIVES

THE ORIGINS OF CHRISTMAS

Today, people disagree about whether Christmas was based on winter solstice celebrations. Many believe Christians copied Roman festivals to make Christmas more popular. But Pastor Keven DeYoung says there is no evidence that early church leaders tried to blend Christian and pagan holidays. He says the church was trying to "transform the paganism of the Roman world" rather than copy it. DeYoung also says that according to ancient tradition, it would have made sense for Jesus's conception to take place on March 25 because that was near the date of the spring equinox, which marks the beginning of spring. Early Christians believed it was the date when God created Earth.

time, Constantine was emperor of Rome. In 312 CE, he converted to Christianity and made it Rome's national religion. The pope at the time, Pope Julius I, chose the date of December 25 for Christmas. Church leaders knew Saturnalia was popular. They may have thought they could increase the popularity of Christmas by having it during solstice celebrations. They may have hoped Christmas would replace pagan holidays.

THE SPREAD OF CHRISTMAS

Some religious scholars say the Christian church did not want to be associated with pagan festivals or customs. Christian leaders didn't want Christianity confused with other religions. But despite this, many traditions stuck. One hundred years later, Christmas spread to Egypt. By the 500s CE, the holiday had reached England. By the 700s CE, it had traveled north to Scandinavia.

Many people celebrated Christmas much like they celebrated the winter solstice. They decorated their homes, burned Yule logs, and feasted. Gift giving came to symbolize the gifts given to Jesus by the three Magi.

THE ADVENT SEASON

Another Christmas tradition that developed over time is Advent. For Christians, the weeks leading up to Christmas are marked by Advent. It's unknown when exactly Christians first started observing Advent, but it is mentioned in writings from the 300s and 400s CE.

Advent is a time to reflect on Jesus's coming. It is observed on the four Sundays before Christmas. Each week during Advent, a special candle is lit. The candles are often placed inside a wreath. On Christmas Eve, a fifth and final candle is lit. The candles burn to celebrate Jesus's birth.

STRAIGHT TO THE
SOURCE

The birth of Jesus is depicted multiple times in the Bible. The following passage from the Gospel of Luke contains imagery commonly depicted in Christmas Nativity scenes:

While [Joseph and Mary] were [in Bethlehem], the time came for the baby to be born, and she gave birth to her firstborn, a son. . . .

And there were shepherds living out in the fields nearby, keeping watch over their flocks at night. An angel of the Lord appeared to them, and the glory of the Lord shone around them, and they were terrified. But the angel said to them, "Do not be afraid. I bring you good news that will cause great joy for all the people. Today in the town of David a Savior has been born to you; he is the Messiah, the Lord. This will be a sign to you: You will find a baby wrapped in cloths and lying in a manger."

Source: "Luke 2: New International Version." *Bible Gateway,* 2011, biblegateway.com. Accessed 4 May 2023.

CONSIDER YOUR AUDIENCE

Adapt this passage for a different audience, such as the readers of a newspaper. Write a news article conveying this same information for the new audience. How does your article differ from the original text and why?

CHRISTMAS OVER TIME

Over time, Christmas became a more popular holiday. For many people across Europe, Christmas was a time for music, feasting, and rowdy celebration. Some modern Christmas traditions and symbols began at this time. One was the Christmas tree.

The tradition of decorating Christmas trees began in Germany. Evergreen trees were important symbols in winter solstice celebrations. This is because they stayed green

At Windsor Castle, Queen Victoria and Prince Albert decorated Christmas trees with ornaments, gifts, candles, and gingerbread. They also decorated trees for the royal staff.

even in winter, when other trees lost their leaves. The Germans were the first to decorate evergreens with candles, candies, and gifts at Christmastime.

One family made the Christmas tree famous worldwide. The United Kingdom's Queen Victoria and her husband, Prince Albert, were both of German heritage. In 1848, the *Illustrated London News* published an illustration of the royal family standing around their decorated Christmas tree. This illustration made Christmas trees incredibly popular.

CHRISTMAS GINGERBREAD

One popular Christmas tradition is decorating gingerbread houses. This became popular in the early 1800s. It was influenced by the Brothers Grimm fairy tale "Hansel and Gretel." In this story, a witch lures two children to a house made of gingerbread and sweets. Baking and decorating gingerbread was already a common Christmas activity in Europe. But the story inspired bakers to make their decorations more detailed and impressive. Soon, people enjoyed creating and decorating their own fairy-tale gingerbread houses.

The Puritans had strict religious beliefs and practices. They disliked the pagan origins of Christmas and thought the holiday's festivities were too rowdy and disorderly.

CHRISTMAS IN AMERICA

Not everyone participated in Christmas celebrations. In 1644, Puritans in England banned Christmas. They were a pious religious group. They believed Christmas celebrations were inappropriate and distracted people from religious worship. Some Puritans emigrated to what is now the United States. In 1659, they banned Christmas in Massachusetts. This ban lasted until 1681.

Christmas wasn't popular in the United States until around the mid-1800s. In 1870, it became the first federal US holiday. This means it is officially recognized by the US government.

PERSPECTIVES

BANNING CHRISTMAS

The Puritans of the Massachusetts Bay Colony believed Christmas went against their religious beliefs. They disapproved of Christmas festivities such as dancing, drinking alcohol, and gambling. They believed these activities led to sin. They also thought the festivities distracted people from religious worship. An early law book details the Puritan law banning Christmas. It says, "Whosoever shall be found observing any such day as Christmas or the like, either by forbearing of labor, feasting, or any other way . . . shall pay of every such offence five shillings."

SANTA CLAUS

One popular Christmas symbol is Santa Claus. He is based on Saint Nicholas, a real person who lived in the 300s CE in what is now Turkey. He was the saint of school children. For the Dutch, December 6 was Saint Nicholas's feast day. On this day, children received gifts.

The Dutch brought this tradition to the United States. One famous description of Santa comes from the 1823 poem "A Visit from St. Nicholas," by Clement Clarke Moore. It is also known

In the late 1800s, cartoonist Thomas Nast created 33 Christmas illustrations for *Harper's Weekly*. Most of them featured a jolly, white-haired Santa. These illustrations helped create the modern image of Santa.

as "'Twas the Night Before Christmas." Other beliefs and tales about Santa became popular over time. In some modern stories, Santa lives at the North Pole. He has a workshop where elves make toys. He also keeps a list of which children have been naughty or nice.

THE CHRISTMAS SPIRIT

The book *A Christmas Carol* played a big role in how people thought about Christmas. It was written by Charles Dickens and published in England in December 1843. It is about Ebenezer Scrooge, a greedy old man

The first edition of *A Christmas Carol* was published with colored illustrations by John Leech. Copies of the book sold out in just a few days.

who is visited by three ghosts on Christmas Eve. They are called the Ghost of Christmas Past, the Ghost of Christmas Present, and the Ghost of Christmas Yet to Come. The ghosts show Scrooge scenes from his life and the impact of his actions on others. This inspires him to change his ways.

Dickens's message was about forgiveness and family. The book was popular and revived the Christmas holiday in England and the United States. It focused the true meaning of Christmas on charity and generosity.

STRAIGHT TO THE
SOURCE

In 1823, Clement Clarke Moore wrote a poem known as "'Twas the Night Before Christmas." The modern character of Santa Claus comes primarily from Moore's poem:

A bundle of Toys he had flung on his back,
And he looked like a pedler just opening his pack.
His eyes—how they twinkled! his dimples how merry!
His cheeks were like roses, his nose like a cherry!
His droll little mouth was drawn up like a bow
And the beard of his chin was as white as the snow;
The stump of a pipe he held tight in his teeth,
And the smoke it encircled his head like a wreath;
He had a broad face and a little round belly,
That shook when he laughed, like a bowlful of jelly.
He was chubby and plump, a right jolly old elf,
And I laughed when I saw him, in spite of myself.

Source: Clement Clarke Moore. "A Visit from St. Nicholas." Academy of American Poets, n.d., poets.org. Accessed 8 Mar. 2023.

POINT OF VIEW

This passage describes Santa Claus. How is this version of Santa Claus different from Saint Nicholas, and why? How are they similar and why? Write a short essay explaining what you find.

CHRISTMAS TODAY

T oday, Christmas is still a religious holiday. Christians continue to celebrate Christmas by attending church services, lighting Advent candles, and reflecting on Jesus's birth. But many people celebrate Christmas in nonreligious ways too.

In 2019, 93 percent of Americans celebrated Christmas. More than 80 percent of non-Christians celebrated Christmas with nonreligious traditions. These might include decorating trees, hanging Christmas lights,

During the holiday season, many people decorate their homes with colorful electric lights. Some set up extravagant Christmas light displays.

Many people bake cookies around Christmastime, especially gingerbread and sugar cookies. These are often cut into festive shapes and decorated with frosting and sprinkles.

baking cookies, or watching holiday movies. Popular Christmas movies include *Rudolph the Red-Nosed Reindeer* and *How the Grinch Stole Christmas.*

Some modern Christmas traditions, such as feasting, can be traced back to winter solstice celebrations. Today, popular Christmas foods include cookies, gingerbread, ham, turkey, potatoes, and stuffing. Another popular Christmas treat is eggnog, a creamy drink made from milk and eggs. Many people drink eggnog only at Christmastime. Lots of

Christmas traditions have changed over time. Many are a combination of different cultures and customs. Some are based in religious liturgy. Others are not.

Modern traditions include sending Christmas cards, filling stockings, and opening Advent calendars. Like regular calendars, Advent calendars mark the days leading up to Christmas. They include numbered doors that can be opened each day. Behind each door is a Bible verse or small treat, such as a chocolate or piece of candy.

CHRISTMAS CARDS

In 1843, Henry Cole sent the first Christmas card. Cole was a famous supporter of the arts. Because he had so many friends, he received many letters. It was considered rude not to answer mail. To save time, Cole had a card designed with an illustration. The card was printed to say, "A Merry Christmas and A Happy New Year To You." Cole made thousands of copies and sent them to his friends. Many people copied him. The tradition of sending Christmas cards stuck. Modern Christmas cards often include photos of family, children, or pets.

CHRISTMAS TRADITIONS

 Christmas tree

 Stockings

 Advent candles

 Feasting

 Yule log

 Santa Claus

 Gift-giving

 Baking cookies

 Christmas lights

 Christmas cards

Over time, many traditions have become associated with Christmas. Think about the origins of these Christmas traditions. What do these traditions have in common?

CHRISTMAS GIVING

The custom of gift giving has existed since the very first Christmas celebrations. But it was not a large focus of the holiday until around the 1900s. The legend of Santa Claus made gifts a bigger part of Christmas.

Over the years, Christmas also became much more commercialized. This means people spend

The Christmas season is one of the busiest times of year for shopping malls, department stores, and other major retailers.

huge amounts of money during Christmastime. Many businesses make enormous profits off the holiday. The United States even has specific days dedicated to Christmas shopping. In November, many businesses have sales on Black Friday and Cyber Monday, which follow Thanksgiving Day. Many people spend these days hunting for deals or discounts on Christmas presents.

They might shop online or in stores. Some stores even start selling Christmas decorations and merchandise as early as October.

Companies may also offer special holiday products that people can only get at Christmastime. For example, Starbucks offers seasonal drinks in holiday-themed cups. Many musical artists also put out albums of Christmas songs or perform at Christmas concerts.

Today, people spend more money on Christmas than ever before. In 2022, the average American spent at least $1,000 at Christmastime.

PERSPECTIVES

HOLIDAY BLUES

For many people, Christmas is a holiday full of happiness and memories. But it can also be a stressful, exhausting time of year. For people suffering from mental illnesses, Christmastime can increase depression and anxiety. This is known as the holiday blues or holiday depression. According to psychologist Michelle Paul, the holiday blues can be brought on by "too high or unrealistic expectations for what things 'should' or 'must' be."

For some people, this means Christmas can end up feeling frustrating and superficial. Some people think Christmas has turned into a holiday that is only about gifts. Buying gifts can be expensive and stressful. Many people believe Christmas should be celebrated in more meaningful ways.

Christmas has long been celebrated as a mix of religious and secular traditions. Ways of celebrating the holiday have changed throughout history. Traditions continue to evolve. Today, Christmas is one of the most popular holidays in the world.

EXPLORE ONLINE

Chapter Five explores how Christmas has evolved into a modern holiday. What is the main point of this chapter? What key evidence supports this point? Go to the article about Christmas at the website below. Find a quote from the website that supports the chapter's main point.

WHAT IS CHRISTMAS?

abdocorelibrary.com/christmas

IMPORTANT DATES

c. 2500 BCE
Stonehenge is built. People in the Northern Hemisphere celebrate the winter solstice.

c. 500s
Livy writes about Romans celebrating Saturnalia.

c. 4
Jesus is born in Bethlehem.

336 CE
The first Christmas celebration takes place in Rome under Emperor Constantine.

1659
The Puritans ban Christmas in the Massachusetts Bay Colony.

1823
Clement Clarke Moore's poem "A Visit from St. Nicholas" is published.

1843

Charles Dickens's *A Christmas Carol* is published. It becomes an instant hit.

1848

The *Illustrated London News* publishes an illustration of Queen Victoria and Prince Albert decorating their Christmas tree. Christmas trees become popular.

1870

Christmas becomes a federal holiday in the United States.

STOP AND
THINK

Tell the Tale

Chapter One of this book describes a family celebrating Christmas. Imagine that you are celebrating Christmas with friends or family. Write 200 words about what Christmas traditions you participate in. What sights, sounds, and smells do you experience?

Dig Deeper

After reading this book, what questions do you still have about Christmas? With an adult's help, find a few reliable sources that can help you answer your questions. Write a paragraph about what you learned.

Why Do I Care?

Maybe your family does not celebrate Christmas. Maybe you celebrate different winter holidays. But that doesn't mean you can't think about how Christmas applies to you. Should people care about holidays that are different from their own? Does knowing about the history of Christmas make you more knowledgeable about your own traditions?

You Are There

This book discusses solstice festivals such as Yule and Saturnalia. Imagine you are celebrating the winter solstice. Write a letter home telling your friends about the sights, smells, and sounds you experience. What do you notice about the festivities? Be sure to add plenty of detail to your notes.

GLOSSARY

ancestor
a family member from whom a person is descended

charity
the act of caring for those in need

conception
the moment when a pregnancy first begins

equator
an imaginary line around the middle of the Earth

liturgy
a practice of worship

Nativity
a visual representation of the birth of Jesus

nostalgic
having fond feelings for the past

pagan
relating to religious beliefs that are not part of main recognized religions

pious
extremely religious or devoted to religious beliefs

pope
the head of the Catholic church

secular
not associated with religion

superficial
existing on the surface level, or not particularly meaningful

ONLINE RESOURCES

To learn more about Christmas, visit our free resource websites below.

Visit **abdocorelibrary.com** or scan this QR code for free Common Core resources for teachers and students, including vetted activities, multimedia, and booklinks, for deeper subject comprehension.

Visit **abdobooklinks.com** or scan this QR code for free additional online weblinks for further learning. These links are routinely monitored and updated to provide the most current information available.

LEARN MORE

McKenzie, Caroline. *The Ultimate Kids Christmas Book.* Hearst Home Kids, 2023.

Utnik-Strugala, Monika. *Christmas Is Coming.* NorthSouth, 2021.

INDEX

About the Author

Emma Kaiser is a writer and educator based in western Minnesota. She has an MFA in creative writing from the University of Minnesota. Her writing has appeared in a number of publications. She is the author of four other nonfiction books for students.